# My First Birthday

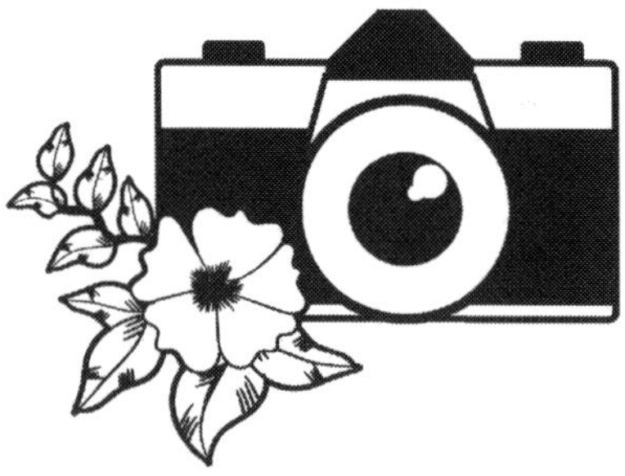

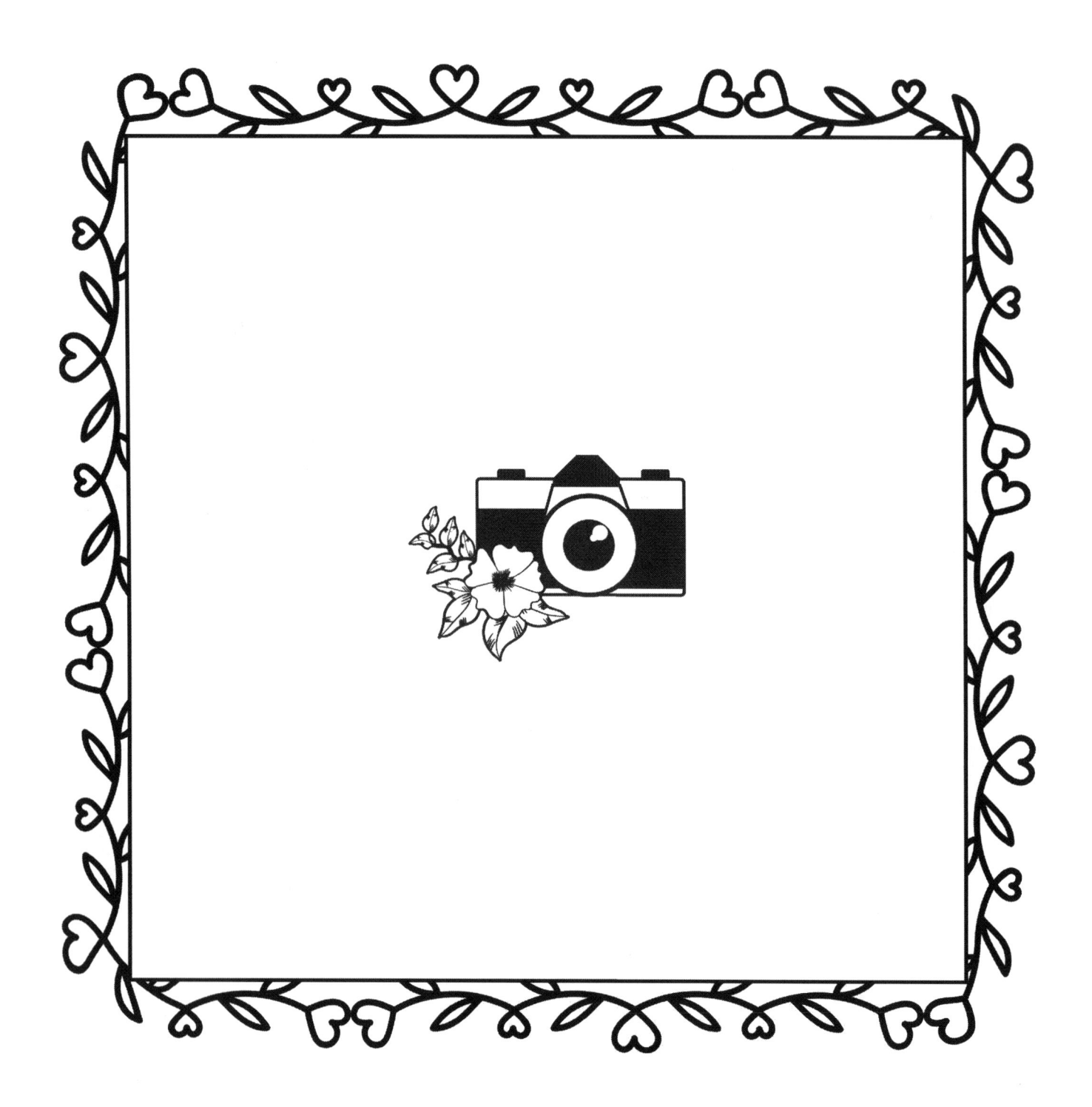

*My name is*

..............................................................................

*I was born on*

..............................................................................

*and this is*

*My First Birthday*

*Memory Book*

# My Gifts

From :

From :

From :

From :

From :

From :

From :

From :

# My Gifts

From:

From:

From:

From:

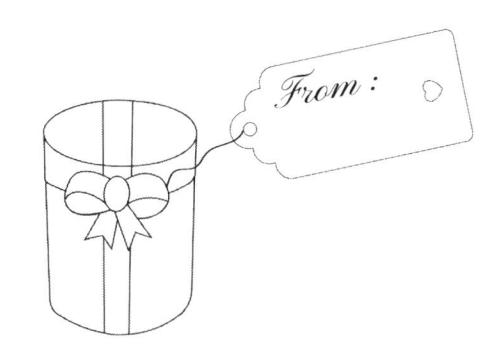

From:

From:

From:

From:

# My Gifts

From :

..................................................

From :

..................................................

From :

..................................................

From :

..................................................

From :

..................................................

From :

..................................................

From :

..................................................

From :

..................................................

# My Gifts

From :

From :

From :

From :

From :

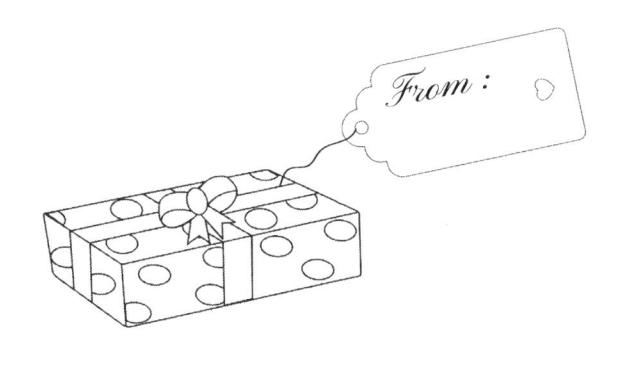

From :

From :

From :

Printed in Great Britain
by Amazon

Printed in Great Britain
by Amazon